Otters

Written by Adrienne Mason

Illustrated by Nancy Gray Ogle

KIDS CAN PRESS

WILDLIFE SERIES

Kids Can Press

For Ava and Patrice—DH
To my sister, Lori, and my brother-in-law Randy—NGO

I would like to thank Dr. Jane Watson, Malaspina University College, Nanaimo, BC, for manuscript review and consultation. Thanks also to Stacey Roderick for her careful editorial work and pleasing manner that make working with Kids Can such a joy. Finally, thank you to Valerie Wyatt for ten years of expert editorial massage on several of my writing projects and a seemingly endless supply of encouragement and support.

Kids Can Press acknowledges the financial support of the Ontario Arts Council, the Canada Council for the Arts and the Government of Canada, through the BPIDP, for our publishing activity.

Published in Canada by
Kids Can Press Ltd.
29 Birch Avenue
Toronto, ON M4V 1E2

Published in the U.S. by
Kids Can Press Ltd.
2250 Military Road
Tonawanda, NY 14150

www.kidscanpress.com

Edited by Stacey Roderick
Designed by Marie Bartholomew
Printed and bound in Hong Kong, China, by Book Art Inc., Toronto

The hardcover edition of this book is smyth sewn casebound.
The paperback edition of this book is limp sewn with a drawn-on cover.

CM 03   0 9 8 7 6 5 4 3 2 1
CM PA 03   0 9 8 7 6 5 4 3 2 1

National Library of Canada Cataloguing in Publication Data

Mason, Adrienne
    Otters / written by Adrienne Mason ; illustrated by Nancy Gray Ogle.

(The Kids Can Press wildlife series)
Includes index.

ISBN 1-55337-406-1 (bound)
ISBN 1-55337-407-X (pbk.)

1. Otters — Juvenile literature. I. Ogle, Nancy Gray
II. Title. III. Series: Kids Can Press wildlife series.

QL737.C25M38 2003   j599.769   C2002-902990-2

Kids Can Press is a *Corus*™ Entertainment company

Contents

Otters

Otters are active animals that live in or near water. They are sometimes seen romping on land or rolling in the water. Otters are carnivores. This means they eat other animals for food. Their closest relatives are weasels and badgers.

Otters have a thick coat of fur to help them stay warm, even when they are wet.

Otters are mammals. Mammals breathe air using their lungs, give birth to live young and most have furry bodies. Mammals are also warm-blooded. This means that their body temperature stays about the same, even when the temperature outside changes.

Kinds of otters

There are two kinds of otters in North America:
the river otter and the sea otter.

A river otter has a long body and a long tail. Its head is quite flat
and pointed. An adult male river otter weighs from 7 to 14 kg
(15 to 31 pounds). A female is a bit smaller and weighs from 5 to
11 kg (11 to 24 pounds). River otters live in water and on land.

Sea otters are much larger than river otters. An adult male can weigh as much as 43 kg (95 pounds). That is as heavy as a large dog. A female sea otter weighs about 15 to 31 kg (33 to 68 pounds). Sea otters live only in the ocean.

OTTER FACT

River otters and sea otters live for about 10 to 20 years. Female otters usually live longer than males.

Where otters live

River otters are found in most parts of North America. They live near streams, lakes or the ocean. River otters hunt for fish and other food in water. Their homes — called dens — are on land.

Sea otters live in the Pacific Ocean. They are usually found in coastal areas, near to land. Sea otters are sometimes seen where a large seaweed, called kelp, grows. The seaweed gives them a place to hide and to find food.

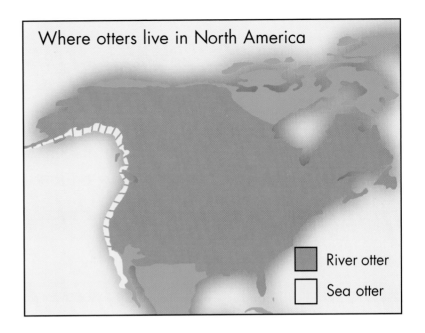

Where otters live in North America

■ River otter
□ Sea otter

Otter bodies

An otter's body is built for life on water and on land. This sea otter spends most of its time in the sea, but it can walk awkwardly on land.

Ears and Nose

Strong muscles close an otter's ears and nose to keep out water when it dives.

Teeth

Powerful teeth and jaws help an otter crunch the shells and bones in its food.

Lungs

Extra-large lungs give the otter enough air for long dives underwater.

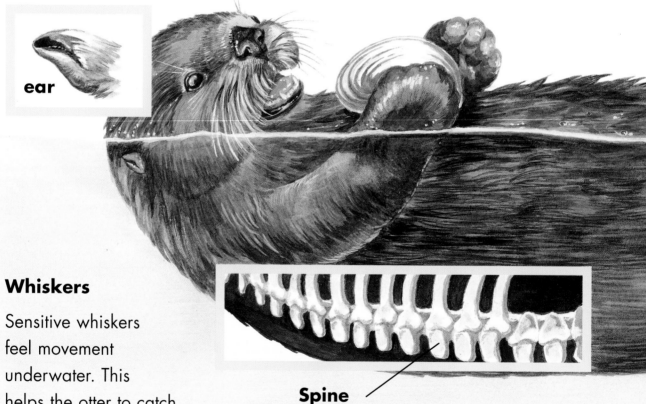

ear

Whiskers

Sensitive whiskers feel movement underwater. This helps the otter to catch food. Whiskers help the otter find food even when the water is muddy.

Spine

A flexible spine allows the otter to twist and roll. This means it can clean and fluff all of its fur, even that in the middle of its back.

Paws and claws

Sensitive paws help an otter find and catch prey underwater. Sharp claws stop the food from getting away once it is caught.

Fur

An otter has two kinds of fur. Guard hairs on the outside of its coat are flat and long. These hairs shed water. A thick layer of short, fine hairs traps air next to the otter's skin. This layer is called the underfur.

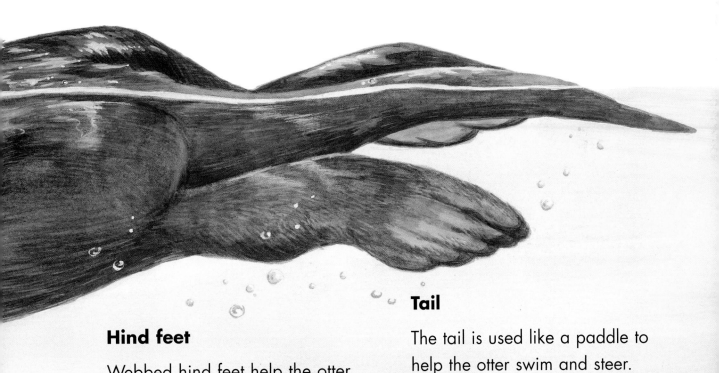

Hind feet

Webbed hind feet help the otter swim. A sea otter's hind feet are so large they look like flippers.

Tail

The tail is used like a paddle to help the otter swim and steer.

Keeping clean

An otter must have clean fur to survive. Air trapped in clean, fluffy underfur helps keep an otter warm in cold water. The air bubbles form a layer that keeps water away from the otter's skin. Dirty, matted fur cannot trap the air bubbles.

An otter uses its sharp claws to comb and fluff its fur. This is called grooming. Grooming helps get dirt out of the fur. It also traps the air bubbles in the underfur.

An otter can also blow air into its fur. Mother otters sometimes blow air into the fur of their babies.

A sea otter's skin is quite loose. This allows the otter to grab a flap of skin and pull it around to the front of its body for grooming. A flexible spine also helps the otter reach all parts of its fur.

Sea otter fur is so thick that there can be up to 1 million hairs in a piece of fur the size of a postage stamp.

How otters move

Otters always seem to be on the move. They are good swimmers and divers, and river otters often frolic on shore.

When an otter dives, it tucks in its front paws and kicks its hind feet like swim fins. Strong muscles help the otter push forward in water.

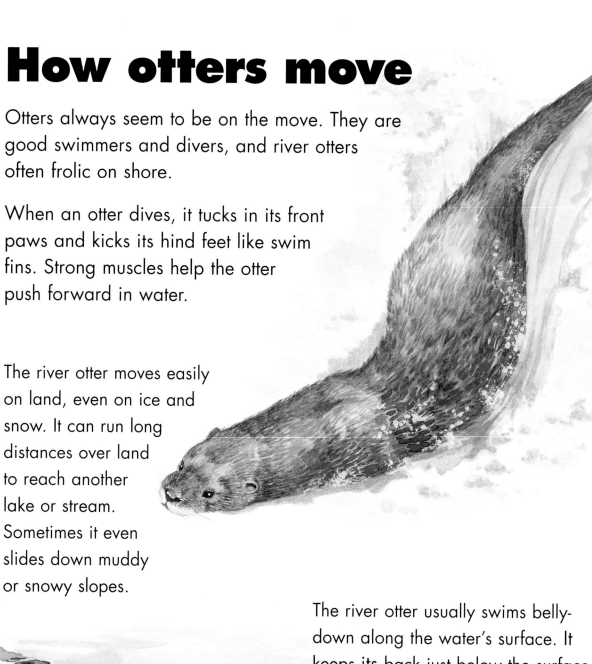

The river otter moves easily on land, even on ice and snow. It can run long distances over land to reach another lake or stream. Sometimes it even slides down muddy or snowy slopes.

The river otter usually swims belly-down along the water's surface. It keeps its back just below the surface so all you can see is its head.

The sea otter swims along the water's surface on its back. It kicks its hind feet out to the sides or swishes its tail to keep moving. A mother otter will often carry her babies with her as she swims or dives. A sea otter can stay under water for as long as four minutes.

The sea otter is very clumsy on land. Its flipper-like hind feet are great for swimming but hard to use on land. When a sea otter does come ashore, it usually stays close to the water's edge. It may come ashore to rest or if it is sick or injured.

Otter food

Otters eat other animals. The animals an otter eats depend on where it lives.

OTTER FACT

Sea otters must eat a lot to help them stay warm in the cold ocean. They eat about one-quarter of their body weight each day.

River otters can swim fast enough to catch fish. Fish is their favorite food. They also eat frogs, insects, crayfish and even mice or birds. River otters bring their food to shore to eat.

Sea otters eat a variety of marine creatures including sea urchins, snails, squid, crab and occasionally fish. A sea otter eats in the water while floating on its back. It sometimes carries a stone on its chest and uses it to smash open hard shells.

Otter homes

River otters usually hunt in the water, but they rest in dens on land. They also have their young in dens. Sometimes river otters use old beaver lodges or hollow trees for dens. They can also take over the burrows of other animals in the bank of a stream or lake.

Sea otters do not have a home like a river otter's den. Instead, they stay in areas of the ocean where there is food and shelter from storms. Sometimes they live in forests of kelp. Kelp forests calm the crashing waves. There is also a lot of otter food in kelp forests.

River otters sometimes travel far inland searching for food. They often use the same trail over and over again.

19

Otters and their young

Otters give birth to live babies. Baby otters, called pups, feed on their mother's rich milk.

Sea otter babies are born in the water. Babies can be born at any time of year, although they are often born in spring or early summer. Mothers usually have only one pup at a time. The pup is born with its eyes open. It cannot swim but is so fluffy that it floats.

The mother sea otter carries the pup on her chest or back until it learns to swim on its own. She brings food to the pup and grooms its fur.

River otters give birth in the spring. The mother otter moves into a den where she has one to six pups. Pups are born helpless, with their eyes closed. Their eyes stay closed for three weeks. River otter pups start learning to swim when they are about six weeks old.

Sometimes a mother sea otter will wrap the pup in kelp to keep it in one place while she dives for food.

How otters grow and learn

Pups stay with their mother for as long as a year. They follow their mother and learn how to swim, dive, catch food and stay safe. Mothers also teach their young how to groom their own fur.

When they are ready, the pups leave their mother. In a year or more, they will find mates and have their own babies.

Otters use grunts, coos, hisses and whines to "talk" to one another. Pups are the noisiest and often squeal loudly when left alone. They are calling for an adult.

Young otters play and wrestle with one another. This looks like fun, but it also teaches important survival skills. Play-fighting is practice for when otters really do have to fight.

How otters protect themselves

River otters use musk—a scented oil that is stored under the tail—to mark their territory. They are strong fighters and will attack animals that enter their territory. River otters will even sneak into beaver dens or muskrat burrows to fight them. Bobcats, lynx, coyotes and wolves all hunt river otter. Mothers must protect the pups from eagles, owls and even some types of large fish.

Sea otters have fewer enemies. They must watch for killer whales and sharks, and bald eagles can attack the pups. If enemies are near, a mother will tuck her pup under her front legs and dive. Sea otters often stay in large groups, called rafts, for protection. They also hide in kelp forests.

Large rafts of sea otters can have up to 200 animals.

If sea otters are scared, they raise their paws and hiss.

25

Otters and people

Long ago, sea otters were hunted for their fur.
People used the fur to make coats. Today there are
laws that protect the otters from hunters, but they are
still in danger from oil spills. Even a small spot of oil on
its fur can keep the otter from staying warm. Otters also
need healthy oceans for their food supply.

Many people work hard to protect the habitat of otters.
They try to make sure that oceans, lakes and rivers stay
clean and healthy. When otters get oil in their fur after an
oil spill, people help clean and wash them. Aquariums also
help otters get healthy again.

River otters need watery places to survive. People sometimes drain these wet areas or pollute rivers and lakes. When this happens, river otters lose their habitat — their shelter and food.

Otters around the world

Here are some of the otters that live in other parts of the world.

Africa

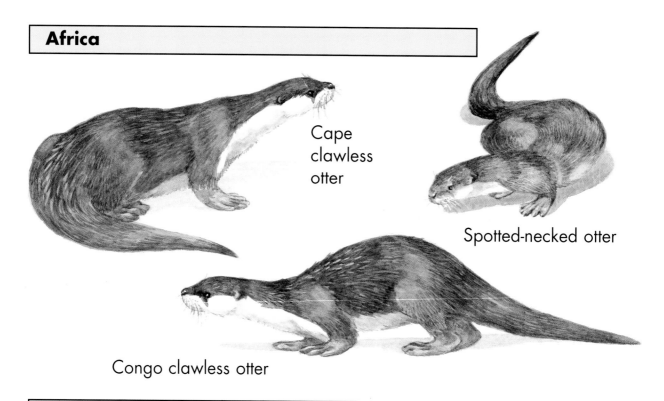

Cape clawless otter

Spotted-necked otter

Congo clawless otter

Asia

India smooth-coated otter

Oriental small-clawed otter

Hairy-nosed (or Sumatran) otter

Asia, Europe and Africa

Eurasian otter

OTTER FACT

It was thought that the hairy-nosed otter of Asia did not exist anymore, but in 1998, three pups were found.

South America

Sea cat (or marine otter)

Southern river otter

Neotropical otter

Giant otter

Watching for otters

Since river otters also hunt for food in the ocean, people sometimes confuse them with sea otters. Here is what to look for to help you decide which kind of otter you are looking at:

• If the otter is running or being very active on land or on a dock, it is a river otter.

• If the otter looks as big as a German shepherd dog, it is probably a sea otter. Sea otters are very large—about two or three times bigger than river otters.

• If the otter is swimming on its belly, it is probably a river otter. Sea otters usually rest or swim on their backs. They sometimes hold all four legs out of the water.

You can also look on land for these other river otter signs.

• The tracks on this page are life-sized. How do your hands compare?

• Look for river otter slides on the banks of rivers or lakes.

• Scat is the name for otter droppings or body waste. River otter scat usually has pieces of bone or shell in it.

Words to know

carnivores: animals that eat other animals

den: an underground home for otters

grooming: cleaning fur by combing and fluffing it

guard hair: the stiff, long hairs on the outside of an otter's fur

habitat: the place where an animal naturally lives and grows

kelp: a large, brown seaweed

mammal: a warm-blooded animal whose babies are born live and fed mother's milk

musk: a scented oil stored in glands under a river otter's tail

pup: a baby otter

raft: a large group of sea otters

underfur: a thick layer of fine hairs next to the otter's skin

warm-blooded: having a warm body temperature, even when it is cold outside

Index